FRYDERYK
CHOPIN

Richard Tames

Franklin Watts
London ● New York ● Sydney ● Toronto

Contents

© Franklin Watts 1991

First published in Great Britain
in 1991 by
Franklin Watts
96 Leonard Street
London EC2A 4RH

First published in the USA by
Franklin Watts, Inc.
387 Park Avenue South
New York, N.Y. 10016

First published in Australia by
Franklin Watts
14 Mars Road
Lane Cove
NSW 2066

UK ISBN: 0 7496 0480 8

Phototypeset by: JB Type, Hove, East Sussex
Printed in: Belgium
Series Editor: Hazel Poole
Designed by: Nick Cannan

A CIP catalogue record for this book is available from
the British Library.

Warsaw

He had a French name, his father was French and he spent almost half of his life in France, but no-one ever doubted that Chopin was Polish. His music drew on the peasant tunes and dances of his native land and became an inspiration for his troubled country. When he later died in exile, some Polish soil was put on his grave.

Chopin's father, Nicolas, came from the Vosges, on the eastern border of France. He had been a **wheelwright** who prospered, bought a vineyard and went into wine-making. But Nicolas was restless for adventure. When a friend wrote asking him to join him in his tobacco business in Poland he went. The country was on the eve of extinction at the hands of its more powerful neighbours and Nicolas

Nicolas Chopin — tobacco-dealer, soldier and French teacher — father of a musical genius.

Chopin's mother, Justyna, who took in boarders to support the family income.

got caught up in the dramatic events of the day. Despite his slight stature, he served with distinction in the Polish National Guard during the doomed uprising of 1794 and rose to the rank of Captain. Afterwards he made his way into aristocratic circles as a teacher of French, the second language of the Polish nobility.

In 1802, Nicolas Chopin was appointed tutor to the children of Countess Skarbek, who lived on an estate at Zelazowa Wola, about 30 miles from Warsaw, the Polish capital. In 1806 he married Tekla-Justyna Krzyzanowska, who was companion and lady-in-waiting to the Countess. Their daughter, Ludwika (Louise), was born the following year and in 1810 they had a son, whom they christened "Fryderyk Franciszek Szopen" (Frederic François Chopin in the French language).

A 20th century impression of Chopin's boyish brilliance at the keyboard.

That same year, the Chopin family moved from Zelazowa Wola to Warsaw so that Nicolas could take up a new position as a professor of French at the Warsaw Lyceum. To support his growing family — Isabella was born in 1811 and Emilia in 1813 — Nicolas took on further teaching work at two military academies and a college for Catholic priests. Justyna also took in some of his students as boarders as a further boost to the family income — which meant plenty of young friends for the Chopin children.

Like Mozart, the young Chopin began to play the piano by interrupting his elder sister's lessons. Soon they were playing duets. Recognising his son's talent, Nicolas sent him for lessons with Adalbert Zywyny, a Czechoslovakian violinist, pianist and composer. The older man soon realised that the six year old was a child of exceptional abilities and proceeded to give him a broad and thorough training. He introduced him to the works of the German masters, from Bach to Beethoven, as well as to the more fashionable composers of the day, like the brilliant piano virtuoso Kalkbrenner.

Fryderyk began to compose his own works even before he knew enough about music to write them down for himself. Zywyny would write down his compositions for him. The first, a **polonaise**, was published in 1817. A march which he composed soon after appealed so much to the Russian Grand Duke Constantine (the ruler of Poland) that he had it scored so that his military band could play it during parades. In 1818, the boy made his first public performance at a charity concert in the palace of the prominent Radziwill family. At the age of 11, he appeared before the visiting Tsar Alexander I, improvising on a new invention — a piano-organ called the aeolo-melodicon. The Tsar presented him with a diamond ring to mark the occasion.

By the time the boy was 12, Zywyny knew there was nothing more he could teach him. So he sent him to Josef Elsner, who was *an accomplished composer and founder of the newly-established Warsaw Conservatory. The boy was also enrolled at the Lyceum, where his father taught, to complete his academic education.

During his summer holidays, the frail teenager was sent to Szafarnia in the country for the good of his health. In the village, at festivals and weddings, he would hear traditional Polish folk music. The toe-tapping dances remained a lifelong influence and he wrote over 50 mazurkas.

Graduating from the Lyceum, Chopin decided not to go to university but to proceed with a career in music. Elsner gave him every encouragement, believing him to be nothing less than a genius. Elsner exerted a decisive influence on Chopin's future by advising him to concentrate on composing rather than playing:

"The ability to play an instrument perfectly — as Paganini does the violin or Kalkbrenner the piano — with all that this ability implies ...

Niccolò Paganini (1782–1840), violin virtuoso, sketched by Ingres.

is still only a means to arrive at the expression of thought. The celebrity which Mozart and Beethoven enjoyed as pianists has long since evaporated ...”

Chopin repaid Elsner's faith with hard work. When he was not actually studying or practising, he could be found at concerts or the opera. Chopin's first trip abroad was a brief visit to Berlin in 1828. There he had the opportunity to introduce himself to Mendelssohn who was only a year his senior but already a famous composer. But Chopin was too shy to go forward and meet him. His second trip took him to Vienna, the musical capital of Europe, where he gave two highly successful recitals. These included some of his own compositions and an improvisation on a traditional Polish drinking-song, which brought a tumultuous response from the audience.

Chopin inherited his father's slightness of stature, never weighing as much as 100lbs and was always troubled by poor health.

But the man within was strong in his passions and, as a youth, he was often led by them. It was at about this time he fell hopelessly in love with the **soprano** Konstancja Gladkowska, a fellow-student. But he loved from afar, not daring to tell her of his devotion. In a letter to his friend, Titus Woyciechowski, the young composer frankly confessed his helplessness:

“You cannot imagine how sad Warsaw is to me ... Oh, how bitter it is to have no one with whom one can share joy and sorrow, how dreadful to feel one's heart oppressed ... Six months have passed and I have not yet exchanged a syllable with her of whom I dream every night. While my thoughts were with her I composed the Adagio (slow movement) of my concerto and early this morning she inspired the Valse (waltz) which I send along with this letter.”

In 1830, Chopin gave two public concerts in Warsaw at which he played two piano concertos of his

Chopin was never at ease in concerts and preferred a salon audience, as here at Prince Esterhazy's home.

own composition. He was now an established local celebrity. But Vienna had shown him what might be possible. Could he progress any further in his own country? Or would he have to go to one of the great centres of European music to develop his talent to its limit?

All his life Chopin suffered from indecisiveness. Sometimes the decisions which caused him problems were entirely trivial ones — like which jacket to wear. Sometimes they were major ones — which country to live in? And often it was someone else or circumstance that made the decision for him.

In November 1830, Chopin decided that he had progressed as far as he could in Warsaw. He set off for Vienna, where he had already enjoyed much success. Almost as soon as he arrived he heard that a great revolt had broken out in Poland against Russian rule. Should he go straight back to join the fight as his father had done a generation before? His family wrote to urge him to stay where he was, saying he was "not strong enough to bear the hardships and fatigue of a soldier's life." Nevertheless he hired a carriage and drove back along the road to Warsaw. But his decisiveness did not last. As he travelled he came to realise that his family was right. So he turned round and went back to Vienna.

Chopin soon found that the Viennese people had already forgotten all about him. He gave a couple of concerts but entirely failed to repeat his former success. He did manage to hear a great deal of music performed and composed several pieces of his own, but after eight months it became clear that he was getting nowhere and he decided at last to move on to Germany.

Arriving in Stuttgart, Chopin learned that the great Polish uprising had completely failed. Russian troops were in the streets of Warsaw. There could be no going back now.

The city Chopin outgrew — Warsaw, capital of Poland and the scene of his first public success.

Chopin's Paris

When Chopin arrived in Paris in 1831, it was the most turbulent and brilliant city in Europe. The revolutions of 1830-31 had placed a new king, Louis Philippe, on the throne of France and flooded his capital with refugees and exiles from the failed uprisings in Poland and Italy.

Chopin himself, though largely unaware of political and social issues, was powerfully impressed by the striking contrasts between the city's rich and poor: "You find here the greatest splendour, the greatest filth, the greatest virtue and the greatest vice ... there is shouting, uproar, noise and mud past anything you can imagine. You can get lost in this swarm ... no one enquires how anyone else manages to live..."

In the salons of the wealthy and fashionable, leading political figures mixed with artists and writers, bankers and businessmen, to plot, to flirt, and to be seen and talked about against a background of gossip and music. Ill at ease on the concert platform, Chopin felt almost relaxed among the cultivated and the cultured. Although he was to travel extensively on occasion, Paris was to remain his real home for the rest of his life.

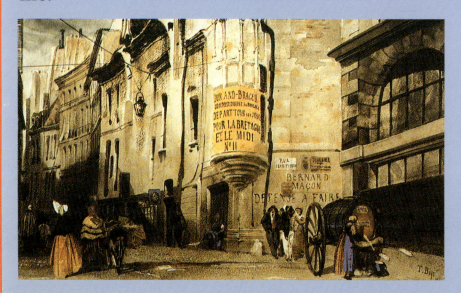

Louis Philippe (above) **styled himself as "King of the French" rather than King of France, a gesture to democracy. His capital, Paris** (left), **was home to many more than the French — and especially to the Polish.**

Exile

Chopin arrived in Paris in September 1831 — just in time for the great cholera **epidemic**. Fortunately he escaped infection, but for a short while he endured some hardship and began to suffer from what he dryly called "consumption of the purse".

Armed with written introductions, the young virtuoso made the acquaintance of Cherubini, head of the Conservatoire and the most influential musical figure of all of France. Thanks to him Chopin soon got to know other major musical figures such as Rossini, the most popular operatic composer of that time, and the dazzling concert pianists, Liszt and Kalkbrenner, from whom he took

The Hungarian Franz Liszt (1811–86) was an established star pianist at 15 and was to publish 1,300 works.

lessons for a short while.

In February 1832, Chopin gave a concert in the Salle Pleyel, a small hall owned by a famous maker of pianos. Financially the event was a failure, not even covering its expenses, but it made Chopin a man to be talked about. A second concert in May strengthened his reputation and once he had been accepted by the Rothschild banking family he was well and truly established. Fashionable and wealthy young ladies flocked to take lessons from the charming and immaculately dressed newcomer.

Although he was later to learn how to sell his compositions for a good price, Chopin would always have to rely on teaching for his regular income. He was far too much of a perfectionist to be able to turn out music just because he needed to pay his bills. Besides, he actually liked teaching and was good at it, although he left behind him no new method of teaching the piano and, indeed, no outstanding student.

Chopin was to become one of music's specialists. Unlike Mozart, who could turn his hand from string quartets to full-scale operas, Chopin concentrated all his efforts on a single instrument — the piano. His mastery of it was complete. He

A "daguerreotype" (early photo-graph) of Chopin. This method of photography was invented by Frenchman Louis Daguerre in 1835.

understood the range of its possibilities and the skills required to bring them out more than any previous composer. Chopin's famous Etudes (studies) are the accomplishment of a gifted artist who was also a great technician. Each one is a carefully designed exercise intended to teach a particular technique, but each is also an admirable composition which can be enjoyed for its own sake. Appropriately they are dedicated to Liszt, whose playing Chopin himself greatly admired. There is, however, no such thing as a Chopin symphony or Mass. Although he wrote three **sonatas** and two concertos he was essentially a miniaturist and his most characteristic compositions are in unusual forms which he did not invent but made very much his own — the ballade, nocturne, fantaisie and prelude.

In Paris, Chopin could enjoy the company of a wide circle of brilliantly accomplished acquaint-ances — the composers Bellini and Mendelssohn, the singer Pauline Viardot-Garcia, the musicians Hummel and Franchomme, the painter Delacroix and the Polish poets Mickiewicz and Witwicki. Personal friendships and artistic admiration did not, however, always go together. Chopin liked Berlioz, but not his music. The same was true of Robert Schumann, whose reviews of Chopin's concerts were so generous that the composer actually complained about them — "He exaggerates so much he makes me look ridiculous."

As well as stimulating company, Chopin enjoyed the comforts and conveniences that came with success. He dressed in black velvet waistcoats and **patent leather** shoes. His rooms — always in an apartment far from noise, smoke and dirt — were full of flowers and pictures and books. He spent money as fast as he earned it, but for him luxuries were necessities, as he explained to a friend:

"I move in the highest circles, among ambassadors, princes and ministers ... it is for me an absolute necessity, for thence comes, so to speak, good taste ... You will imagine that I must have made a fortune by this time; but the **cabriolet** and the white gloves eat the earnings almost entirely, and without these things people would deny my good form."

In 1835 Chopin travelled to the fashionable German health resort of Karlsbad to see his parents. It was to be their last meeting, though neither side could know that at the time. In the course of his journey the composer also visited the Wodzinskis, exiled aristocrats whom he had known in Poland. Attracted to their daughter, Maria, he joined them again the following summer in Marienbad, proposed marriage and seemed to have been accepted. However, with Chopin's failing state of health, possibly from consumption, there was family

pressure placed upon Maria, and her secret engagement was quietly dropped.

Youthful Maria Wodzinska — the love that was not to be. Chopin came to rely on strong-willed women to organize his life.

Wearing distinctive Polish caps, a young couple tread a stately polonaise or polacca, a folk dance promoted to the ballroom and much favoured by Chopin (facing page).

George Sand 1804-76

When Chopin met her, George Sand was the most notorious woman in France. Famous for her novels and infamous for her love life, she seemed to go out of her way to defy convention and flout respectable opinion. A passionate spokeswoman of the right of women to live as freely as men, she sometimes emphasised her arguments by dressing in men's clothes and smoking cigars.

Christened Amantine Aurore Lucile Dupin, she was brought up by her aristocratic grandmother at Nohant in provincial Berry, 200 miles south of Paris. Even as a child she read widely, though her formal education was limited to two years at a fashionable English convent school in Paris. The death of her grandmother left her mistress of a small estate and quite well off at the age of 17. To please her mother, however, she married Casimir, Baron Dudevant, a local nobleman whose main interests turned out to be hunting, drinking and other women.

In 1831, Aurore deserted her husband in favour of Paris and a career as a writer. Her first novel, *Indiana,* was published in 1832 under the **pseudonym** of George Sand — half borrowed from her current lover Jules Sandeau. It told the story of a woman who leaves an unhappy marriage to find true love. It made her instantly famous and set the style for many more books combining the same themes of personal revolt and the wrongs done to women.

By the time she met Chopin, George Sand had been through a highly publicised divorce, and her writing had also entered a new phase, focusing on the problems of the poor. Despite her devoted attachment to the composer she still found time to continue writing throughout their eight years together.

In 1848, when her relationship with Chopin came to an end, Sand edited a radical magazine.

But after the failure of the 1848 revolution to establish a new social order she returned to live quietly at Nohant, writing gentle and highly moral stories of rural life. By the time of her death she had completed over 100 works and was admired by authors as distinguished and different as the Russian Turgenev, the Italian Mazzini and the Americans Emerson and Whitman. She died, in striking contrast to her rebellious middle years, a pillar of respectable society.

A caricature of George Sand, smoking and wearing trousers in the "shocking" phase of her life. Later she became a pillar of respectability.

Possessed

Late in 1836, Chopin was introduced to Aurore Dudevant, better known by her pen name as "George Sand". They disliked each other on sight. He was slight, shy and intensely conservative in dress and manners. She was bold, brash, eccentric and contemptuous of convention. Chopin remembered later "I did not like her face ... There is something off-putting about her." Over the following months, however, the forceful novelist found herself strangely but strongly attracted to the elegant, retiring musician. Genius of any_ kind fascinated her, and she also had a genuine interest in music. The novelist Balzac's account of her shows just how powerful an impact she could make:

"I found Comrade George Sand in her dressing-gown, smoking an after-dinner cigar, in front of her fire in an immense room. She had on lovely yellow slippers ornamented with fringe, bewitching stockings and red trousers ... She has not a single white hair in spite of her frightful misfortunes; her swarthy complexion has not changed; her lovely eyes are as brilliant as ever ... She leads the same life as I do. She goes to bed at six in the morning and gets up at noon ... It is a man she would like to be ... She will be unhappy always ..."

In 1838, Sand decided that Chopin needed a winter in the sun to restore him to health. She decided on the Spanish island of Majorca and whisked Chopin away with her two young children, Maurice and Solange, in tow. While the fine weather lasted all was well, but when it grew cold, Chopin's condition worsened so alarmingly that it was rumoured he was developing tuberculosis and their landlord threw them out for fear of infection. They ended up in a couple of rooms in a run-down monastery in the mountain village of Valldemosa. Damp, under-fed and miserable, they also had to endure the hostility of the local people, who were scandalised that they were not married. Constant rain, loneliness and the lack of even a decent piano drove the composer to the edge of despair. His protectress once "found him at 10 o'clock at night before his piano, his face pale, his eyes wild and his hair almost standing on end. It was some minutes before he could recognise us." Chopin's health was all but broken by the time they left the island in February 1839, and it took three months of careful nursing in Marseilles before he was well enough to move on to the Dudevant home at Nohant to spend the summer convalescing. After that they returned to Paris, where they took separate houses in the same street.

Chopin returned to the concert platform in 1841. His first engagement was a small-scale recital at Pleyel's. The reviews were excellent — "Chopin has done for the piano what Schubert has done for the voice." The second concert involved the composer's close friends, the celebrated cellist Franchomme and the mezzo-soprano Pauline Viardot-Garcia. The critics' praise was even more extravagant — "sheer poetry superbly translated into sound." Chopin was also invited to play for King Louis-Philippe at the Tuileries Palace.

These public appearances were extremely well-rewarded financially. Chopin's reputation saw to that. But he found them a great strain on his nerves as well as his strength. Unlike Liszt, who could literally break the insides of a piano with his thunderous technique, Chopin

The Tuileries palace provided the sort of elegant setting in which Chopin felt appreciated — and was well rewarded.

was renowned for the delicacy of his touch. It was a style much more suitable for a small, quiet circle of admiring friends, than for a vast concert-hall and an anonymous audience whose attention must be caught or lost. The composer himself readily confessed his fears:

"I wasn't meant to play in public ... Crowds intimidate me, their breath stifles me, their stares petrify me, their strange faces throw me into confusion ..."

Each summer Chopin and Sand returned to Nohant. Restored by

The composer absorbed in his work — an amateurish but convincing sketch by George Sand captures Chopin's power of concentration.

fresh air and the undemanding pace of country life, comforted by the companionship of friends, and freed from the distraction of teaching, Chopin could find the time and energy to compose some of his finest works. Ever the perfectionist, he worked slowly, constantly polishing and refining his compositions. Compared to Bach or Beethoven, or even the short-lived Schubert, his total output was very limited; but each item that he produced was beautifully crafted and almost all have stood the test of time and endless performance by hands far less sensitive than those of their composer.

Sand appeared to many to mother Chopin devotedly, freeing him from everyday worries and anxieties so that he could give himself entirely to his music. She certainly understood his weaknesses very well and knew that he:

"Never contemplated without dread the idea of leaving Paris, his doctor, his friends, his room, even his piano. He was a slave to habit and every change, however small it might be, was a terrible event in his life."

But, as a creative artist herself, George Sand could not suppress her own strong personality, and the situation was further strained by the jealousy which her growing son, Maurice, felt towards Chopin, who took up so much of his mother's time and affection.

Sand's habit of drawing on her own personal experiences for her writing eventually gave a clear indication of how things were going when she published a novel which unmistakably reflected her unspoken view of her relationship with Chopin. The heroine, an actress called Lucrezia Floriani, is a wonderful mother, devoted to her children. The villain, Prince Karol, whom she has nursed through a near-fatal illness (echoes of the Majorca disaster) destroys her with his jealousy. Chopin read the novel but utterly failed to recognise himself in the destructive and selfish character of Karol.

Sand put her view of the deteriorating situation in a letter to an old friend:

"I have become so weary of passions and so disillusioned that even without effort or sacrifice I have grown old before my time ... I know that many people accuse me, some of having exhausted him by the violence of my senses, others of having driven him to despair by my coldness. I believe you know the truth."

The breaking-point came over Sand's daughter Solange. Mother and daughter quarrelled frequently, and Chopin often took the daughter's side. Solange eventually tried to escape by marrying a sculptor named Clésinger. When the newlyweds visited Nohant they behaved appallingly. Chopin's attempt to make things better between mother and daughter only made things worse. Sand wrote him a letter which he took as his dismissal. What it actually said is no longer known. Chopin showed it only to his friend, the painter Delacroix, who noted in his diary:

"I must admit that it is atrocious. The cruel passions, the long-suppressed impatiences are having their day."

Chopin then destroyed the letter.

In March 1848, Chopin and Sand passed on the stairs at the house of a mutual friend in Paris. Chopin mumbled that Solange had borne a child and that she was now a grandmother. Sand later wrote:

"I pressed his trembling and icy hand. I wished to speak to him; he slipped away."

Maurice Sand (right) **whose resentment of Chopin's demands on his mother helped to drive the couple apart. George Sand** (opposite) **adopted conventional dress as well as conventional opinions in her later life.**

The King of Instruments

The instrument now generally called a piano is, strictly speaking, a "pianoforte" because it can play both soft (piano) and loud (forte). Its tremendous range of sound makes it perhaps the most versatile of all instruments, almost an orchestra in itself and yet capable of the delicacy of a violin.

The forerunners of the piano were the spinet and the harpsichord, keyboard instruments which produced notes by plucking taut strings. The resulting sound was rather "thin" and "tinny" to the modern ear, which is used to the rich, full sound produced by the piano.

The piano makes its notes by striking the string with a hammer. The ingenious mechanism connecting the keyboard and the hammer was invented in 1711 by the Italian Bartolomeo Cristofori. But it took more than 50 years in Mozart's time, before the piano began to challenge the harpsichord. And it was not until the next generation of composers, in Beethoven's time, that a great deal of music came to be written especially for the piano.

During Chopin's lifetime, the piano was improved in important ways which made it more and more attractive to composers and audiences alike. First, the increasing use of iron in its construction made it capable of taking much more punishment at the hands of very physical performers like Liszt. Second, the tone of the piano became fuller and softer as a result of the use of tempered-steel springs and the replacement of leather-covered hammers with felt-covered ones. Third, improvements in the hammer mechanism enabled the same note to be struck twice or more with only a brief interval between each contact. This made it possible for virtuosos to play faster "trills" than ever before. Finally, the combined result of these various changes was to increase the range of the piano from the five octaves which Mozart had known to a full seven octaves, allowing much greater contrasts between high and bass passages. Chopin was the first great composer to take full advantage of these developments and it was more than 50 years before another composer, Debussy, went far beyond what he had done.

State of the art — a Broadwood grand piano displayed at the Great Exhibition of 1851.

The End

Living with George Sand had never been easy for Chopin, but once they had parted he began to decline rapidly, both physically and emotionally. By February 1848, he was too weak to climb stairs on his own. He gave what was to be his last concert in Paris, though on that occasion he did manage to walk to the piano unaided. Two days later a revolution toppled King Louis Philippe and disorder broke out in the streets of Paris.

Disturbed by these dramatic events and with his lessons brought to an end, Chopin accepted an invitation from Jane Stirling, an adoring Scottish pupil six years his senior, to visit Britain. Between Easter and August he was settled in a suite of rooms large enough to hold no less than three grand pianos. He refused invitations to give a major public concert but allowed himself to be wheeled through an exhausting round of private recitals and receptions, including performing before Queen Victoria at the home of the Duke of Sutherland. Delighted though he was to meet such celebrities as Charles Dickens and the opera star Jenny Lind ("the Swedish Nightingale"), he was nevertheless

Jane Stirling, whose well-meaning but bossy attentions may have hastened the composer's decline.

glad to escape to Scotland to recuperate with Miss Stirling's relatives.

From Miss Stirling herself, however, there was seemingly no escape. She adored him and wanted to marry him. Too tired even to compose, he wanted only peace and quiet. Even the raw Scottish air tortured him — "I can hardly breathe. I am just about ready to give up the ghost", he wrote to an old friend. With the need to earn money, he gave concerts in Manchester, Edinburgh and Glasgow. Soon after, he returned to London to make a final public appearance at a charity ball in aid of Polish refugees from another failed revolt. By the end of November he was back in Paris.

Deathly pale and coughing incessantly, Chopin knew by the spring of 1849 that he was dying. He destroyed a number of his unfinished compositions. Later, too weak to finish the task himself, he asked friends to burn the rest. They did not do so. What survived against the composer's wishes shows that he was an excellent judge of his own work. Although of

Edinburgh in the 1840s — a scene of triumph for Jane Stirling but disastrous for Chopin's health.

great interest to musical scholars, the compositions published after his death do not measure up to Chopin's usual standard of excellence.

On the advice of his doctors he moved to Chaillot, on the edge of the city. In June he sent for his elder sister, Ludwika, but she was unable to leave Poland until August. Solange and Clésinger moved to the neighbourhood to be near him. Jane Stirling came from Scotland and discreetly helped to support his failing finances for, too feeble to teach, he no longer had any regular source of income. He managed to compose two last mazurkas but was not able to make legible copies of them.

In September, Chopin moved back into the city and into a new apartment in the Place Vendôme — his ninth Paris address in 18 years. At first he was interested enough to concern himself with the details of its decor and furnishing. But he soon took to his bed and stayed there, growing weaker each day. He died early on 17 October 1849.

At the composer's special request, Mozart's Requiem was sung at his funeral. He was buried in the Père Lachaise cemetery alongside many of Europe's other great artists. A year later a monument, in the shape of a weeping muse with a broken **lyre**, was unveiled there and his grave was scattered with Polish earth. As was his final wish, Ludwika took his heart back to Poland to be buried in the Church of the Holy Cross in Warsaw.

The spacious, gracious Place Vendôme (below) **— Chopin's last address. The romantic monument to Chopin** (right) **in Paris's Parc Monceau manages to suggest the delicacy of the composer's playing.**

Find out More

Important Books

Fryderyk Chopin: Pianist from Warsaw by William G. Atwood (Columbia University Press, 1987)

Chopin's Letters by Frederic Chopin (Dover, 1988)

Chopin: The Man and His Music by James G. Huneker (Dover, 1966)

Frederic Chopin by Franz Liszt (Vienna House, 1973)

Frederic Chopin, Eighteen Ten to Eighteen Forty-Nine by Stephen P. Mizwa (Greenwood, 1983)

Chopin: His Life by William D. Murdoch (Greenwood, 1971)

Chopin: His Life and Times by Ates Ortega (Paganiniana, 1980)

Important Addresses

Metropolitan Museum of Art
Fifth Avenue at 82nd Street
New York, New York 10028

The Music House
73777 U.S. 31 North
Acme, Michigan 49610

Shrine To Music Museum
University of South Dakota
414 East Clark Street
Vermillion, South Dakota 57069

Museum of American History
Smithsonian Institute
14th Street and Constitution Avenue NW
Washington D.C. 20560

Musical Wonder House
18 High Street
Wiscasset, Maine 04578

Yale University Collection of Musical Instruments
15 Hillhouse Avenue
New Haven, Connecticut 72632

Important Dates

1810 Born in Poland
1816 Takes first music lessons
1817 Writes first composition
1818 First public concert appearance
1821 Performs before Tsar Alexander I
1822 Becomes pupil of Josef Elsner
1828 Visits Berlin
1829 First concerts in Vienna
1830 Leaves Poland for Vienna
1831 Arrives in Paris

1832 First concerts in Paris
1835 Falls in love with Maria Wodzinska
1836 Meets George Sand
1838 Spends winter in Majorca
1841 Returns to the concert platform
1847 Relationship with George Sand breaks up
1848 Visits England and Scotland
1849 Dies in Paris

Glossary

Cabriolet   A horse-drawn carriage with two wheels.

Epidemic   A disease that attacks large numbers of people in many places at the same time and continues to spread.

Lyre   A musical instrument similar to a harp.

Patent leather   Highly polished leather.

Polonaise   A Polish national dance.

Pseudonym   An assumed named and, in the case of authors, a pen name.

Sonata   A musical composition of three or four movements, written for piano or for a solo instrument with piano accompaniment.

Soprano   The highest voice range for women.

Virtuoso   A musician who is very technically skilled in the art.

Wheelwright   Somebody who makes wheels and wheeled carriages.

Index

Picture Acknowledgements

The publishers would like to thank the following for their kind permission to reproduce their photographs in this book: Archiv für Kunst und Geschichte, 14; Carnavalet/Bulloz, 10 (bottom); Carnavalet/Lauros-Giraudon, 22; Mansell Collection, 4,5,6,7,8,11,12,20,23,29,31; Mary Evans, frontispiece, 9,10 (top), 15,17,25,27,28; Photo Harlingue-Viollet, 26; Royal College of Music, cover.